After Harunobu.

Plate 2

Plate 1

After Harunobu.

Plate 3

After Harunobu.

Plate 4

LEFT: After Kiyonaga. RIGHT: After Harunobu.

Plate 5

After Utamaro.

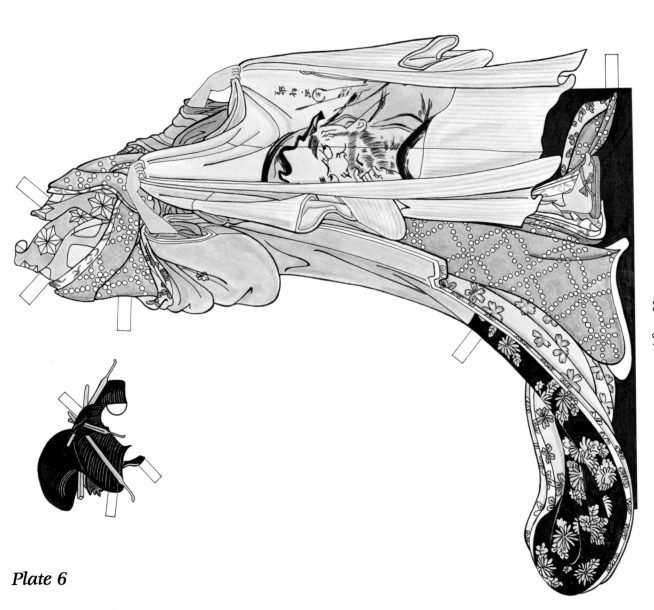

After Utamaro.

Plate 6

After Eisen.

After Eisen.

Plate 7

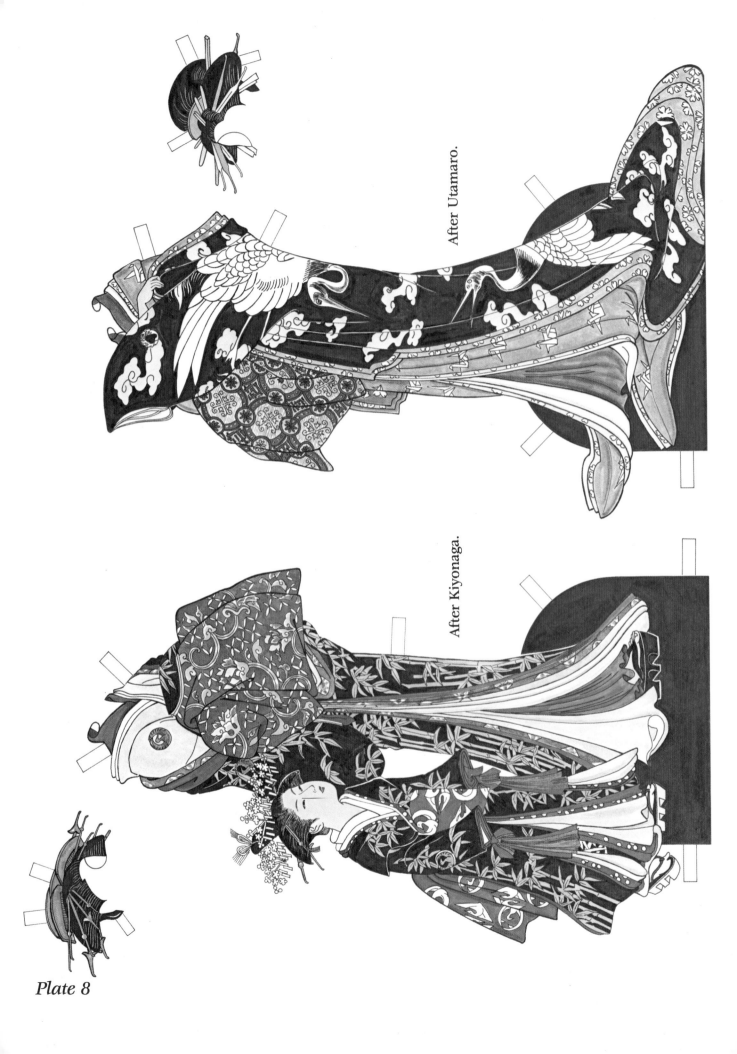

After Utamaro.

After Kiyonaga.

Plate 8

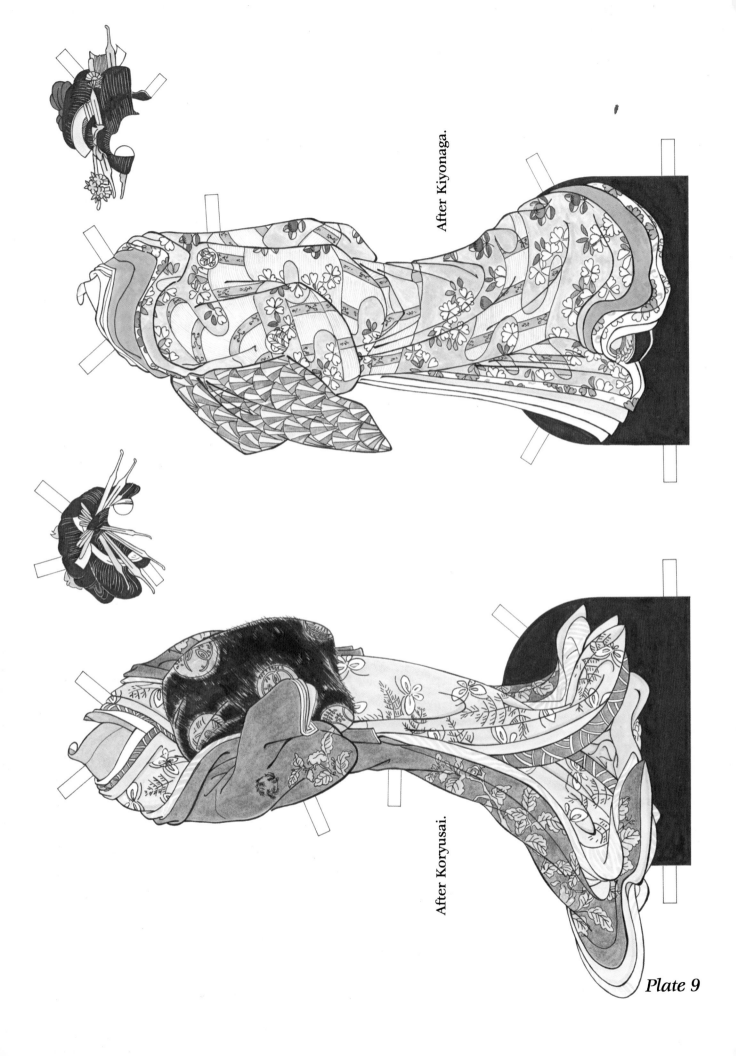

After Kiyonaga.

After Koryusai.

Plate 9

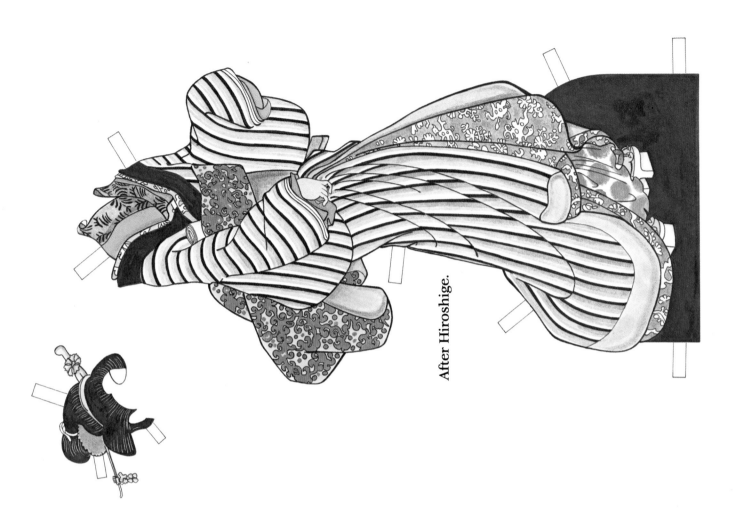

After Hiroshige.

After Kiyonaga.

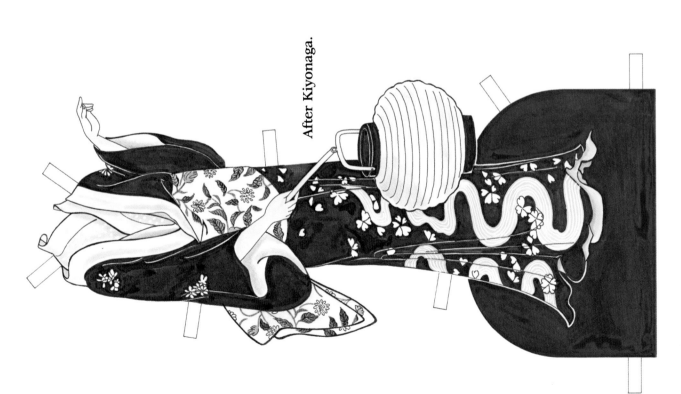

Plate 10

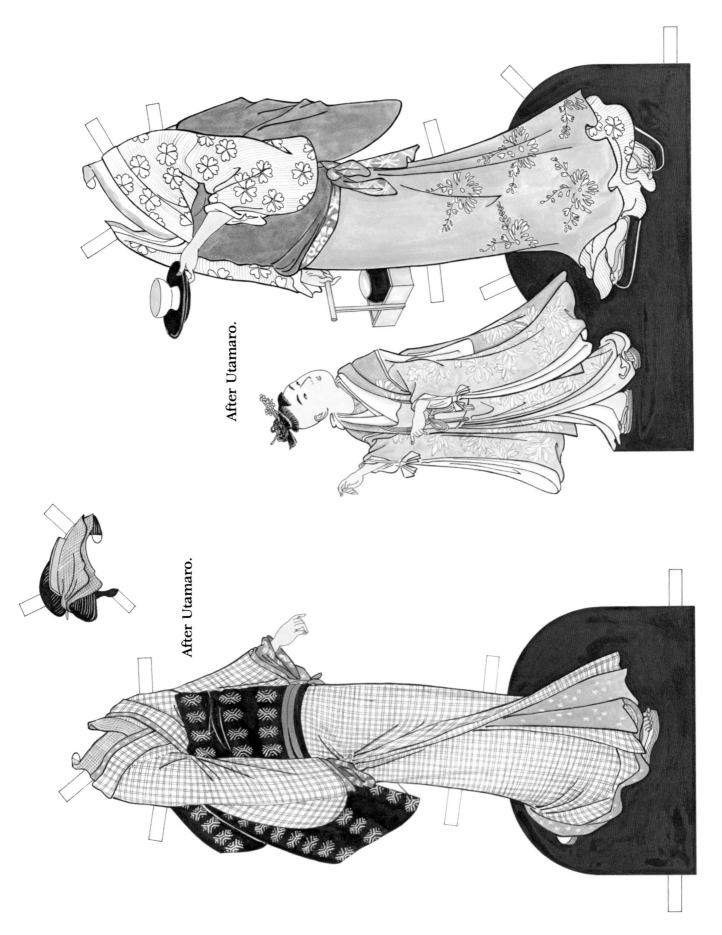

After Utamaro.

After Utamaro.

Plate 11

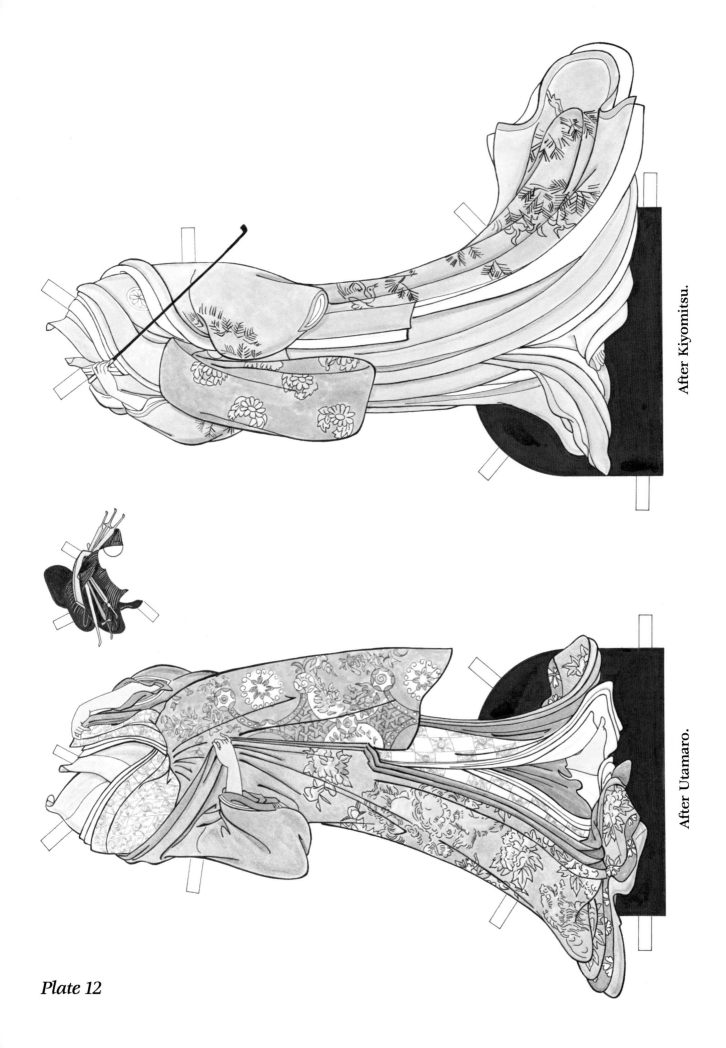

After Kiyomitsu.

After Utamaro.

Plate 12

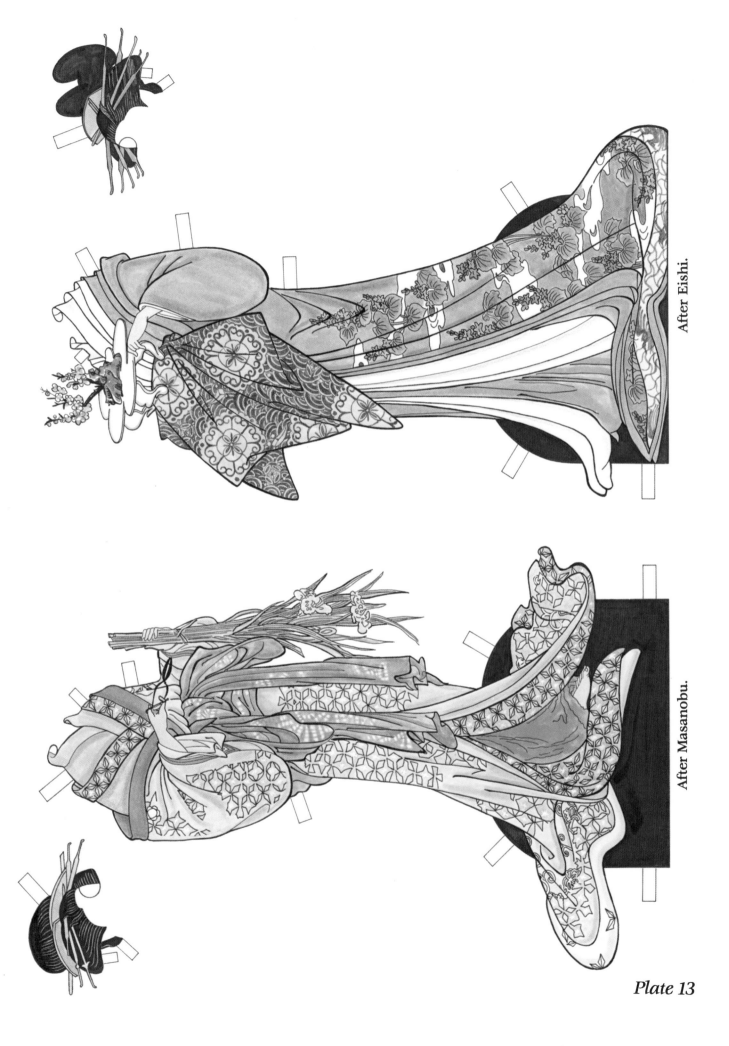

After Eishi.

After Masanobu.

Plate 13

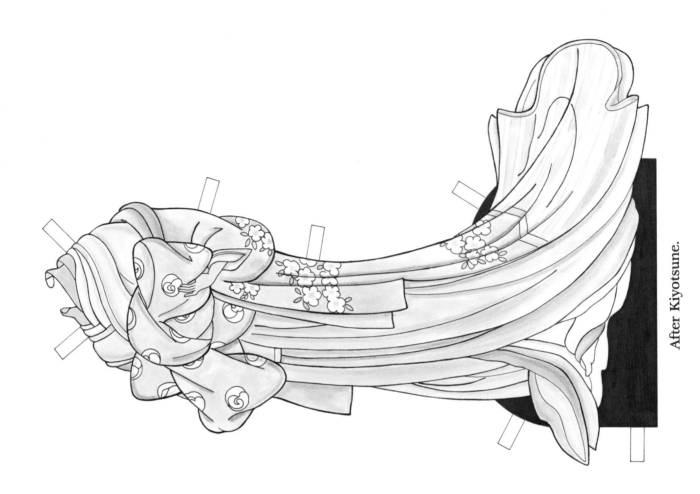

After Kiyotsune.

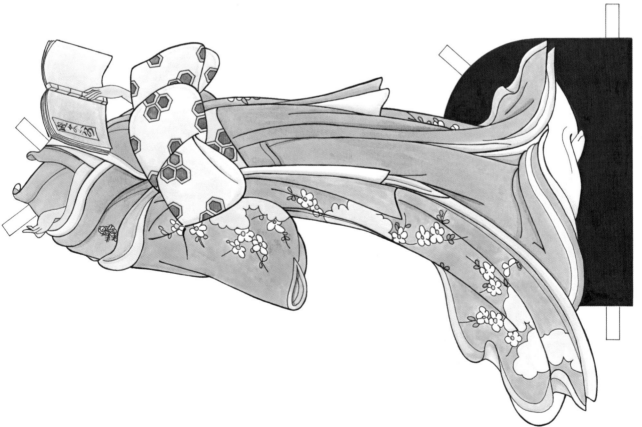

After Harunobu.

Plate 14

After Shigemasa.

After Shigemasa.

Plate 15

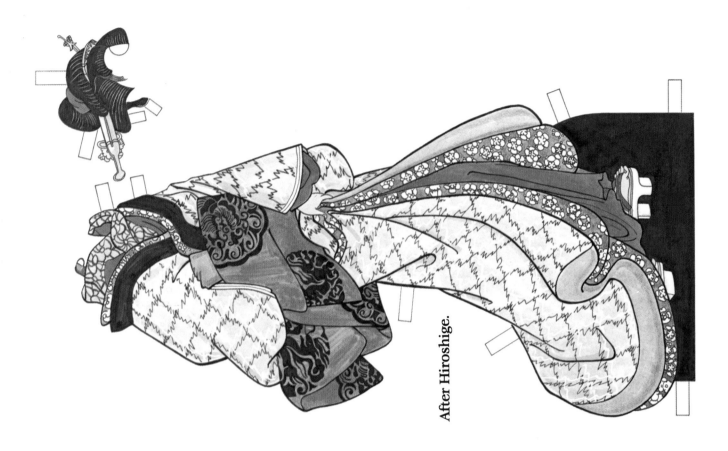

After Hiroshige.

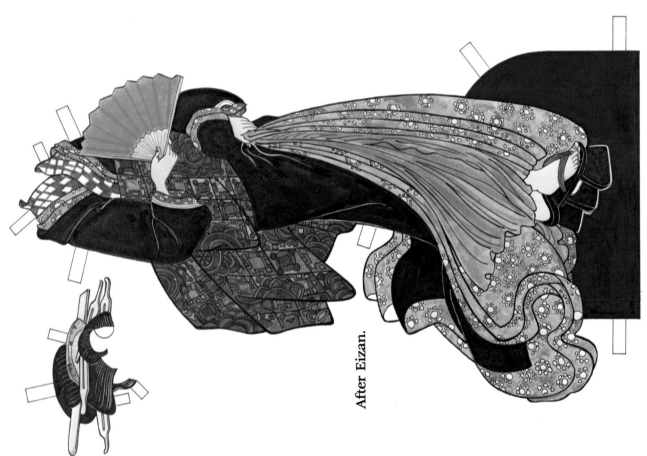

After Eizan.

Plate 16